Robert Shaw-Byrnes has been a successful teacher, university lecturer and schools administrator for several decades. He has turned round failing schools and improved others until they achieved better results and all-round educational outcomes.

Now, in semi-retirement, he is available for consultancy work. Recent commissions have included South Africa, the UAE and in the United Kingdom.

He is currently working on a volume that covers many aspects of school curriculum, teacher training and student enrichment policies.

LIFE SKILLS AND SCHOOL IMPROVEMENT

Robert Shaw-Byrnes

LIFE SKILLS AND SCHOOL IMPROVEMENT

Promoting Success in Education

EMMA
STERN
PUBLISHING

An Emma Stern Publication

Copyright © Robert Shaw-Byrnes 2016

The right of Robert Shaw-Byrnes to be identified as author of this work
has been asserted in accordance with sections 77 and 78 of the
Copyright, Designs and Patents Act 1988.

A CIP catalogue record for this title is available from the British Library.

ISBN: 978-1-911224-10-5

This edition published in 2016

Emma Stern Publishing
107 Fleet Street
London
EC4A 2AB

www.emmastern.com
www.facebook.com/emmasternpublishing
Email: editorial@emmastern.com
Email: marketing@emmastern.com

Printed in Great Britain

This book is a sort of prelude to the main work, to be published by Emma Stern. It is by way of being an introduction to the main themes.

This book is intended to provide support to leaders and teachers in schools, not least those who hope to see improvement. All teachers, at whatever level, are able to inspire colleagues and support them, ensuring that all schools can improve, and through Life Skills and other strategies enable all learners to reach their full potential.

In order to achieve success, it is imperative that there is radical change. If not introduced carefully, this change can lead to dissension and upset, among teachers, learners at all levels, leaders, governors and parents. Indeed, anyone with a stake in the school.

The author combines experience, knowledge and enthusiasm. He has taught successfully on three continents, at secondary and tertiary levels, as well as teacher training in a British university. Shaw-Byrnes has the ability to present ideas and suggestions in a prose style that is readily accessible to all.

'School Improvement is essential reading for all who wish to be a part of making schools fit for purpose in the 21st century.'

INTRODUCTION

Holistic education is the basis of school improvement.

It is grounded on the premise that each learner finds identity, meaning, and purpose in life through connections to:

family

the community

the natural world

spiritual values.

Holistic education aims to call forth from people a reverence for life and a passionate love of learning. This is done, not through an academic curriculum that condenses the world into instructional packages (or subjects) but through direct engagement with family, friends, the school, the community, and the environment. And also leads to examination success. But learners are prepared for Life and not just for examinations.

Introducing Life Skills teaching into schools is a big undertaking. It requires a radical change in teaching methods, and in teachers' attitudes. And the school's Leaders and other stakeholders must change too.

Read what follows and decide if this is what you really want to introduce and promote.

Don't start it and then drop it like a hot potato.

TEACHER AS FACILITATOR

This is vital to change.

Traditional paradigm.

The teacher is the fount of knowledge. He knows the content. The learner is a blank slate (tabula rasa), an empty head to be filled.

Holistic paradigm

The concept of knowledge as a process of reasoning and enquiry.

It requires study skills teaching first.

It demands training and commitment of teachers.

The accumulation of knowledge, not as end in itself, for examinations, but as a process toward self-development.

Requires the breaking down of subject barriers. It is a global approach to learning.

Group work and other forms of collaboration are important.

The personality and skills of the teacher are important. The teacher acts as a guide to finding resources.

Once set up, facilitative teaching is easier than the traditional method.

There is more preparation initially but much less whole-class direct contact. Therefore, less fatigue and burn-out.

CAUTION

Parents need to know what is happening, but not all at once. That is why it might be best to begin with a pilot scheme for one year.

Arguments in favour of teacher as facilitator are many, as we see from the points above, but for parents it is important that they know this method:

* is being phased in gradually;

* leads to better results in external examinations;

* and, therefore, more success at university;

* Life Skills teaching is better for employment prospects.

CHAPTER 1

RECRUITMENT AND INDUCTION OF STAFF

Recruitment

Employing people seems a perfectly straightforward matter: hire them, and then set them to work. Easy.

Easy? Far from it.

Getting the best teachers will cost you time and money. SO.....you need:

* a good recruitment policy in order to recruit suitable employees

* an effective training program

* enthusiastic and credible management and supervision

* to get rid of slackers, moaners, trouble makers and inveterate gossips. (Gossips can do the school a lot of damage.)

The advertisement

Advertise widely. The more potential applicants you reach, the greater the odds are of finding excellent and committed teachers for your school. Many schools make the mistake of running a limited search, and therefore have a limited response. And remember: a good advertisement in many places will serve as an advertisement for the school as well as for a particular applicant. So you are much better off casting a wide net.

This should appear in print media and on your school's website. This advertisement is the first contact with the school, and those not chosen for the short-list must not feel aggrieved.

*****

About the position

We are currently seeking a Head of the Department of English to join a go-ahead primary and secondary school with effect from XXXXX. The Head of Department is responsible for the educational leadership and management of this department. The position requires an experienced educational leader with excellent communication skills and interpersonal empathy and understanding. The successful candidate will have experience working in a similar school context and will also be well-versed in curriculum development and professional development.

About the School

The school is located in a semi-rural area. It is a co-educational day school which was founded 25 years ago. The school takes a student-centred approach to learning. There are currently 480 students, aged 7 to 16 years.

Position requirements

Candidates must have an appropriate first degree and teaching certification. A Master's degree is desirable. Extensive experience of primary and secondary school curricula and programs is required.

The candidate appointed will have successful teaching experience in inquiry methods and trans-disciplinary programs.

Applicants are welcome to contact the school by telephone or email to ask for the application form and other information about the school and its ethos.

The closing date is XXXXXXX. It is hoped to arrange interviews for short-listed applicants within three weeks of this date.

Because of the large numbers expected to apply for this important post in a prestigious school, it will not be possible to contact those who are not chosen for the short-list of candidates. We trust you will understand the reasons for this.

Alternatively, you may prefer to enlist the services of a teacher recruitment company. There are many of these. Be sure to choose a company that is known to provide good service.

Induction

Conducting a well-planned Induction Program for new staff pays many dividends. Use the list below as a guideline.

General introduction to the school. Explain the school's mission, values and policies

If you are serious about providing excellent customer service, then the Induction Program can ensure that this message is provided in a consistent way to all new teachers. Thus, you need to explain:

* Culture of the school and its values

* Proprietor's Vision (if an independent school)

* Policies

Before the first day on the job the new employee needs to know:

* When to arrive

* Where to park

* Whom to report to

* Work station, office materials or other equipment are ready

* Explain hours of work

* Pay Days

* Grooming & dress code

* Vacation time

* Sick leave

* Breaks

* Explain performance evaluation

* Create an employee Handbook

* Ensure that discipline and grievance procedures, which are a part of the contract, are actually there and included in the Employee Handbook.

* Introduce the new teacher to members of staff, including office and ancillary staff.

The basics

* Point out the location of the toilets

* Ditto the staffroom

* Give a tour of the facilities

* Show your new teacher where to store personal belongings

* Explain acceptable treatment of parents – no gossiping.

* Review your policy on Internet and telephone usage in school time

* Smoking policy

* Absences

* Discipline

* Theft

* Absenteeism

* Harassment

* Personal use of equipment and supplies

* Training policies

School security, safety and emergency procedures

* Locking doors and cupboards

* How to call for help

* How to deal with a threatening employee or parent

* Fire procedures

* Personal safety and maintenance of health

* Reporting accidents

Set school expectations

Probationary period and performance appraisal explained.

Review the job description, pointing out what is expected in regard to:

* Duties and responsibilities

* Performance standards

* Hours of work

* Staff meetings

* Workload

* Punctuality to work and to classes

* Purpose of 'free' periods.

CHAPTER 2

TRAINING OF TEACHERS

No matter how good a school is, especially in external examination results, and thus demand for places, there is always room for improvement, and most obviously in the ways that teachers respond.

But teachers' responses are largely set and guided by the Management. A slack Head or other senior members of staff will be copied by teachers, and the rot sets in very quickly. Choose your senior staff with the utmost care. Involve all members of the teaching staff in the training program. No exceptions. (Training of ancillary staff is not included here.)

The purposes of training and professional education are:

* to improve motivation – let staff see that the management and senior staff care about all areas, and not merely such things as numbers on the roll, and the levels of fees.

* to identify potential leaders, as needed and appropriate – HODs, senior staff.

* to identify teachers who can be upgraded – from primary to secondary, for example.

* to allow parents, guardians and other stakeholders to see that you are school of first choice.

* to keep all teachers abreast of developments in teaching and delivery, especially in core subjects like English, Maths and Science.

* to improve recruitment of good staff.

WHAT IS A TRAINING PROGRAM?

A Program should be a series of events and not just a one-off event.

Training will vary. Newly-qualified staff (NQTs) will be trained differently from staff who have been in place for years. For NQTs, the initial training can be a part of the Induction Program. Ideally, this will take place before the beginning of term.

Training is directly related to the skills, knowledge, and strategies necessary to do a particular job. It can include:

* teaching staff members new skills,

* exposing them to unfamiliar ideas,

* giving them the chance to practice and get feedback on particular techniques or styles of working with people,

* encouraging them to discuss their work with others.

Every single member of staff can benefit from training, no matter how experienced they are.

DOES YOUR SCHOOL NEED A TRAINING PROGRAM?

The answer is YES.

All schools – or indeed any company or business – need a training program. The reasons for this assertion will be made clear.

First, such a program shows that the management is serious about

the school's progress and in an individual teacher's progress in the profession.

Stakeholders and parents need to know that the school's Management is serious. In a small town, village or suburb, word goes round quickly, so make sure parents know what is happening in training and education.

A school with a good reputation increases the number of applicants for jobs. Good news travels fast. (So too does bad news, so beware.)

Having the proper training boosts teachers' confidence in their ability to do their jobs.

Ensures that NQTs and staff changing jobs become proficient quickly.

If staff members are given information, and a sound contract, they cannot credibly cost the school time, money and bad publicity with job tribunals.

Experienced staff can suffer burn-out. Good training offsets this.

* It increases their knowledge by introducing them to the latest research, theory and practical methods.

* It keeps them from becoming bored and stale.

* it helps them to maintain interest in and enthusiasm for their work.

* It can expose them to other practitioners with different - and perhaps better - methods.

* It gives them a reason to stay with the school.

* It keeps the school dynamic and healthy.

* Results improve year or year until you become the school of choice.

WHEN TO RUN A TRAINING PROGRAM

Training for new staff should be conducted as soon as possible after they are recruited.

Staff development should be scheduled as part of the normal operation of the school.

Each session need not involve all staff. Plenary sessions might be once a term.

Ring the changes in order to avoid staleness and routine.

Staff training can be costly in terms of time and money. It is possible to employ an outside company, but it makes financial sense to do it in-house. A poor program is worse than no program at all. So it pays to spend some time getting it right.

WHAT TO INCLUDE IN A TRAINING PROGRAM

All staff need a measure of support. That support must come from the top – the Proprietor and the Head.

A comprehensive training program will include the following:

* Training and induction for NQTs.

* Training for new staff who may be experienced in the work but not in the particular method or style which your school uses or intends to use.

* Experienced staff who need bringing up to date with recent ideas and research in teaching styles and methods.

* A separate program for ancillary staff, not least how to deal with members of the public and visitors to the school. It is ancillary staff that outsiders first meet, and thus the responses should be such that they do the school credit. Poor Reception harms the school.

WHO SHOULD BE IN CHARGE OF THE TRAINING PROGRAM?

The Head, who has experience as a teacher and as an administrator. This lends credibility to the whole training program. Many Heads are female, of course, and the use of the male form is for convenience, merely.

In place of student or pupil, I have used the term 'learner', to avoid unnecessary repetition or possible confusion.

THE TRAINING PROGRAM

There are 3 major considerations in developing and running a training program.

* Planning

* Methods

* Evaluation

Planning

Prepare the whole program before you start. This might only be a skeleton outline, but you need it.

A certain measure of staff participation in planning and conducting a training program gives staff members' ownership of that program.

Respond to staff members' needs. Make sure that involvement isn't just nominal, but leads to specific workshops, sessions, etc.

Cover the topics that staff members identify as important. Try to incorporate these into your overall program. Some suggestions will be trivial. Have ready a rationale for explaining that not all subjects are relevant to a training program.

Try to arrange the training in ways that keep participants active: discussion groups, etc.

Schedule training around staff member's needs. Try to avoid late afternoon sessions, when some teachers will be caring for their own children. (But remember: teachers do not call the shots. You do!)

One to one training is sometimes necessary. Examples include NQTs, those transferred from another school, or someone returning to the classroom after a long break because of illness or maternity leave.

Methods

General guidelines.

If the training is meant to teach a method or technique, it should be conducted using the method.

Vary presentation methods to keep people interested.

Among the many methods available are:

* Discussion groups or working in pairs.

* Group activities: small-group problem-solving, collaborative projects, etc.

* Multimedia: audio-visual presentations (videos, audio tape, overheads).

* Physical activities: movement, manipulation of materials

* Individual problem-solving

* Role plays and simulation.

* Individual or group research.

* Examination of a paper on an aspect of education.

* Lecture.

* Try outside presenters, perhaps. Invite someone from the Ministry or local authority. Or perhaps the university. Make sure this is publicised.

Some of these suggestions may not be relevant to your school.

Encourage discussion. It is interactive. It also allows you to check your notes for the rest of the session.

Evaluation

It is important to evaluate the success of otherwise of your program.

Don't be afraid to refine the program in the light of experience. If something does not work, drop it.

If you meet with resistance from teachers, try to find the reasons for the resistance. It does not mean you stop the training program, but you need to know why there is resistance. Good planning will obviate resistance, of course.

Program Evaluation Methods

All programs need to be refined in the light of experience. This evaluation will help you and colleagues in the process of refinement.

Predict how you will see this program in the future. This prediction may not be completely accurate -predictions never are – but it will help you to refine the program.

Write a report. Assess the value of each element of the program (using 'Plus', 'Minus', 'Interesting')

How did the staff help, hinder, or generally influence you?

Complete these two sentences.

On this Program there should have been more opportunities for .... because.....

On this Program there should have been less
.... because....

Elements of the program that were so successful they should not be changed in a future program. Make a list.

Which teachers appeared to derive most benefit from the program?

Which teachers appeared to derive least benefit from the Program?

Consider the reasons for this. Write a list. What could you have done to assist these teachers benefit more from the program? Were you surprised about the progress of the program in any way? If so, what surprised you?

Were you surprised by the lack of progress? If so, why?

How did the staff on this program respond? In order to find out:

* Devise a short questionnaire, to be answered anonymously.

* Meet teachers in small groups according to subject.

* Have one-to-one meetings with teachers.

* Encourage openness.

In what ways has this program influenced or changed you? Be honest with yourself.

Think of 3 things that would help to improve this program. This is best done after meeting with staff members and hearing their views.

Devise an Action Plan. Bear in mind all that you have learned about yourself, the participants, and the topics introduced into the program.

And finally, at least in this section:

Think of all those boring courses you have attended through the years. Don't make your program like those.

Don't underestimate the amount of effort you will need to expend in order to succeed, but also think of the rewards.

CHAPTER 3

LIFE SKILLS SOCIAL SKILLS

Human beings are social animals. The connections are many and most take place out of school. It behoves the school to prepare learners for the social life, including the world of work, beyond school.

The best way for learners to develop social skills is to collaborate with others. Social skills include:

* cooperation

* compromise

* decision making

* communicating

* using emotional intelligence

* using constructive criticism

* trusting others

* delivering on promises

* coordinating work

Flexibility

Learners live in a world of rapid change, especially technological change. It is necessary, therefore, to teach learners how to be flexible and able to adjust to changing circumstances.

Initiative

Maturity is founded on initiative—the willingness to present an idea and bring it to fruition. Learners have to set goals for themselves. This is best achieved through the Inquiry Method. This method demands of learners that they know how to:

* plan

* do research

* create

* refine

* make presentations – orally and in writing.

Productivity

Learners need to be productive in a variety of milieu. Working with others – at school, at the university, at work - requires the skills of:

* Goal setting

* Planning

* Research

* Development

* Evaluation

* Revision & refinement

* Application

All these elements require effective Time Management.

LEADERSHIP SKILLS

Leadership is a group of related skills.

Successful leaders:

* take the initiative,

* have strong social skills,

* are flexible,

* are productive.

Successful leaders know how to:

* Identify goals

* Inspire others

* Organize a group so that all members can contribute

* Resolve conflicts

* Encourage the group to reach emotional maturity

EMOTIONAL SKILLS

Affective empathy (emotional empathy)

The capacity to respond with an appropriate emotion to another's mental state.

Cognitive empathy

The capacity to understand another's perspective or mental state.

STUDY SKILLS

These include

1   literacy

2   numeracy

3   technology

Literacy

These will be mainly transactional skills in writing.

Listening   the varieties of Listening

Speaking   formal   and   informal. Presentations. Debating.

The differences between conversation and discussion.

Reading.

Reading for Pleasure.

Reading for a Purpose. Extracting information from a text.

Writing

Letters – formal and informal.

CV

Job application.

Invitations, etc.

Summary & note making skills

Composition.

The many types and their purposes.

NUMERACY

Maths as now taught, but with different emphases for the real world of work. So instead of abstract figures, teach numeracy skills through such topics as business, entrepreneurial skills, household budgets, debt management, and banking

TECHNOLOGY

Mainly ICT skills but anything that relates to cell phones, I pads, etc.

Automotive skills might find a place in this section.

TIME MANAGEMENT SKILLS

Poor time management can be a major source of stress to you and to colleagues. Stress leads to shoddy work. And even to illness.

Time management skills can change your life for the better. But you must be willing to allow change. Without such change, you will get nowhere – or at least, make only a limited impact. Teach these skills to staff, and they will pass them on to learners in 2 ways: by example; and through formal training.

Question routines, habits and assumptions - your own and others. Time management depends on control. Many routines, habits and assumptions are obstacles to control and change.

Be creative. Find different ways of doing things. Invite suggestions from others, who can often see situations more clearly than you, and come up with new ideas.

Assess what efforts and activities are most productive, and which are not. Dispense with those that not productive.

Emails and phone calls are usually major opportunities to improve time management. BUT they can be time wasters. Try to check your messages only at planned times, and avoid continuous notification of incoming emails.

Leaders need to be selective in what they deal with. You cannot do everything alone. Trust other people to get on with tasks. Learn to delegate tasks. If someone has difficulty completing a task, give them training. If this also fails, they are in the wrong job.

Have a plan for each day and try to stick to it.

Allow time for sport and leisure activities.

Make it clear to colleagues when you cannot be disturbed in your office.

Do one job at a time and see it through to the end.

Set a time for meetings to end. Don't allow staff meetings to go on for many hours.

Also set deadlines for a job to be completed.

If there are too many intrusions, find another place to work.

CHAPTER 4

ENRICHMENT OF LEARNERS

Enrichment is the provision of clubs and activities that are not in the normal timetable.

Enrichment is not for the promotion of curriculum. It is extra-curricular, intended to broaden the interests of learners. It is a part of the promotion of Life Skills teaching and activities.

In a boarding school, it is easy enough to find time for enrichment activities, but this is difficult in day schools because quite often parents and learners do not want to return to the campus at weekends or in the evening. And there is sure to be resistance from teachers.

The answer is to find time in the daytime session, in the final period of Wednesday or Friday.

You might wish to allot the whole of Wednesday afternoon to Enrichment activities. There are several arguments in favour of Wednesday. It is in the middle of the week and provides a break from academic studies.

Benefits of Enrichment Activities

They broaden the interests of learners. Research shows that such broadening has a direct beneficial influence on exam results.

It allows the school to strengthen ties with the local community. Such ties are important, and affect enrolment numbers.

Parents and others can help with enrichment activities. Parents come to the school on a voluntary basis to promote their interests.

Learners realise that the school is, or should be, an integral part of the community.

Teachers can promote a special interest, and this assists their motivation.

Provides time for those learners with a special interest.

Suggestions for activities

Voluntary work in the local community.

Learners could assist in a nursery; or do a shift in a hospital.

First Aid

For example: a nurse from the local hospital could run the First Aid Club. They could perhaps take one term, and then children move to a different activity.

Sport

Physical activity is good for the brain as well as the body.

Business Club/Money Sense.

All aspects of basic economics. Make contacts with the bank staff and local businessmen, especially the bank manager who deals with your school overdraft account.

Societies/Clubs

Debating, Geography, Local history, Science, Maths, Chess.

Dancing

Modern and traditional

Drama

Need not cover the whole year. One term is enough to prepare a play suitable for showing to parents and members of the public.

STEM Society: science, technology, engineering and maths.

Art Club

Fine art: drawing, painting, clay modelling, wire sculptures.

Bake Club

Cookery, sewing, embroidery, etc.

Book Club

Literary society for discussion of books.

Debating society

Debates within the school and then with other schools.

Standard letter to parents and guardians

Dear Parent/Guardian

Greetings.

The Enrichment Program at Glenfield School

The Management, Head and staff members of the school are all determined to upgrade the school in many ways. We are aware that this cannot be fully achieved without the cooperation and trust of parents and guardians.

As part of our initiatives, we are implementing a Program of Enrichment Activities. This means a variety of clubs and activities. The enclosed sheet lists these.

We view enrichment as part of the school day and expect full commitment to the sessions that students choose.

There are many ways in which you can be involved. Think about any special skills you have and would like to share with students. This could refer to games and other sporting activities; to cookery and related household skills; or perhaps to proficiency with a musical instrument.

If you wish to help, please contact the Head - personally, by telephone or in writing by email or letter. We want to hear from you.

Thank you.

(signature)

ADDENDUM 1

CONFLICT RESOLUTION

Conflict situations are an important aspect of the workplace, and this includes schools and colleges.

A conflict is a situation when the interests, needs, goals or values of involved parties interfere with one another. It is a common phenomenon in a school. Different stakeholders may have different priorities; conflicts may involve team members, departments, stakeholders.

Often, a conflict may be a difference of perception. This is not always a bad thing: it may present opportunities for improvement within a department or the whole school. Therefore, it is important to understand and apply the appropriate conflict resolution technique.

There are many ways in which the managers of a school or college may deal with a conflict. Only those in place will know the most appropriate way. For an outsider, albeit one with wide experience of dealing with conflict situations, it is only possible to present the advantages and disadvantages of a way of working, along with certain notes of caution. It is best, of course, if the Head or a member of the management is able to recognise possible areas or flashpoints that might lead to conflict, and pursue activities that will defuse a situation.

The suggestions that follow are:

* Intervention

* Collaboration

* Compromise

* Withdrawal

* Accommodation

Intervention

Examples of when intervention may be appropriate

In certain situations when all other, less forceful methods, don't work or are ineffective

When you need to stand up for your own rights, resist aggression and pressure

When a quick resolution is required and using force is justified (e.g. in a life-threatening situation)

As a last resort to resolve a long-lasting conflict.

Warnings

* May negatively affect your relationship with the opponent in the long run

* May cause the opponent to react in the same way, even if the opponent did not intend to be forceful originally

* Cannot take advantage of the strong sides of the other side's position

* Taking this approach may require a lot of energy and be exhausting to some individuals

Collaboration

Also known as problem solving. Collaboration involves an attempt to work with the other person to find a win-win solution to the problem in hand - the one that most satisfies the concerns of both parties. The win-win approach sees conflict resolution as an opportunity to come to a mutually beneficial result. It includes identifying the underlying concerns of the opponents and finding an alternative which meets each party's concerns.

Examples of when collaboration may be appropriate:

* When consensus and commitment of other parties is important

* In a collaborative environment

* When it is required to address the interests of multiple stakeholders

* When a high level of trust is present

* When a long-term relationship is important

* When you need to work through hard feelings, animosity, etc.

* When you don't want to have full responsibility

Advantages

* Leads to solution of the problem

* Ensures a win-win outcome

* Reinforces mutual trust and respect

* Builds a foundation for effective collaboration in the future

* Shared responsibility of the outcome

* You earn the reputation of being a good negotiator

* For parties involved, the outcome of the conflict resolution is less stressful

Warnings

* Requires a commitment from all parties to look for a mutually acceptable solution

* May require more effort and more time than some other methods. A win-win solution may not be evident

* For the same reason, collaborating may not be practical when timing is crucial and a quick solution or fast response is required

* Once one or more parties lose their trust in an opponent, the relationship falls back to other methods of conflict resolution. Therefore, all involved parties must continue collaborative efforts to maintain a collaborative relationship

Compromise

Compromise seeks a mutually acceptable solution which partially satisfies both parties.

Examples of when compromise may be appropriate:

* When the goals are moderately important and not worth the use of more assertive or more involving approaches, such as forcing or collaborating.

* To reach temporary settlement on complex issues.

* To reach expedient solutions on important issues.

* As a first step when the involved parties do not know each other well or haven't yet developed a high level of mutual trust

* When collaboration or forcing do not work.

Advantages

* Faster issue resolution. Compromising may be more practical when time is a factor

* Can provide a temporary solution while still looking for a win-win solution

* Lowers the levels of tension and stress resulting from the conflict

Warnings

* May result in a situation when both parties are not satisfied with the outcome (a lose-lose situation)

* Does not contribute to building trust in the long run

* May require close monitoring and control to ensure the agreements are honoured.

Withdrawal

Also known as avoidance. This is when a person does not pursue her/his own concerns or those of the opponent. He/she does not address the conflict, sidesteps, postpones or simply withdraws.

Examples of when withdrawal may be appropriate:

* When the issue is trivial and not worth the effort

* When more important issues are pressing, and you don't have time to deal with it

* In situations where postponing the response is beneficial to you, for example -

* When it is not the right time or place to confront the issue

* When you need time to think and collect information before you act (e.g. if you are unprepared or taken by surprise)

* When you see no chance of getting your concerns met

* When you would have to deal with hostility

* When you are unable to handle the conflict (e.g. if you are too emotionally involved or others can handle it better)

Advantages

* When the opponent is forcing / attempts aggression, you may choose to withdraw and postpone your response until you are in a more favourable circumstance for you to push back.

* Withdrawing is a low stress approach when the conflict is short.

* Gives the ability/time to focus on more important or more urgent issues instead.

* Gives you time to better prepare and collect information before you act.

Warnings

* May lead to weakening your position; not acting may be interpreted as an agreement. Using withdrawing strategies without negatively affecting your own position requires certain skill and experience

* When multiple parties are involved, withdrawing may negatively affect your relationship with a party that expects your action

Accommodation

Accommodating the concerns of other people first.

Examples of when accommodation may be appropriate:

* When it is important to provide a temporary relief from the conflict or buy time until you are in a better position to respond/push back

* When the issue is not as important to you as it is to the other person

* When you accept that you are wrong

* When you have no choice or when continued competition would be detrimental

Advantages:

* In some cases smoothing will help to protect more important interests while giving up on some less important ones

* Allows you to reassess the situation from a different angle.

* Warnings

* There is a risk of abuse, i.e. one party may constantly try to take advantage of your tendency toward accommodation. Some people see liberalism as weakness. Therefore it is important to keep the right balance and this requires some skill.

* May negatively affect your confidence in your ability to respond to an aggressive opponent.

* It makes more difficult the transition to a win-win solution.

* Some may not like your smoothing response and be turned off.

ADDENDUM 2

EFFECTIVE CLASSROOM MANAGEMENT

The world changes constantly. The attitudes, expectations and responses of learners also change. It is no longer possible, or desirable, for the teacher to go into a classroom and simply demand obedience.

Teaching styles must change accordingly. The teacher is no longer seen as the fount of all knowledge about a subject. We can expect to be challenged more often. Therefore, teaching has to be a cooperative activity, with the learners using IT.

Learners need to be active.

Enquiry is important.

Disruptive behaviour has to be contained. The reasons for it have to be examined. So all teachers have to be aware of how to maintain control in their classes.

It is imperative to develop processes that are conducive to learning.

CLASSROOM MANAGEMENT AS A PROCESS

Classroom management is a means to create an environment that supports and facilitates academic and social–emotional learning.

To achieve this goal teachers must:

develop caring, supportive relationships with and among learners;

organize and implement teaching in ways that optimize learners' access   to learning – this means use of IT;

keep the class actively engaged -use group methods that encourage   learners' engagement in academic tasks;

promote the development of learners' social skills and self–regulation;

use appropriate interventions to assist those with behaviour problems.

Key tasks that teachers must attend to in order to develop an environment conducive to learning. These tasks include:

organise the physical environment;

establish rules and routines;

develop caring relationships;

implement interesting techniques – clear voice; humour as appropriate; respond to incipient discipline problems.

BE POSITIVE. PREVENTION IS BETTER THAN CURE.

Preventative approaches to classroom management involve creating a positive classroom community with mutual respect between teacher and learners. Teachers using the preventative approach offer warmth, acceptance, and support unconditionally - not based on a learner's behaviour.

Fair rules and consequences are established and learners are given frequent and consistent feedback regarding their behaviour. One way to establish this kind of classroom environment is through the development and use of a classroom contract. The contract should be created by both learners and the teacher. In the contract, learners and teachers decide and agree on how to treat one another in the classroom. The group also decides on and agrees to what the group will do should there be a violation of the contract. Rather than a consequence, the group should decide on a way to fix the problem through either class discussion, peer mediation, counselling, or by one on one conversations leading to a solution to the problem.

Preventative techniques also involve the strategic use of praise and rewards to inform learners about their behaviour rather than as a means of controlling learner behaviour Teachers must emphasize the value of the behaviour that is rewarded and also explain to learners the specific skills they demonstrated to earn the reward. Teachers should also encourage learner collaboration in selecting rewards and defining appropriate behaviours that will earn rewards.

FOSTER PROFESSIONAL TEACHER-LEARNER RELATIONS

Some characteristics of having good teacher-learner relationships in the classroom involve the appropriate levels of dominance, cooperation, and awareness of learners.

Teacher's ability to give clear purpose and guidance concerning learner behaviour. Know your subject thoroughly.

By creating and giving clear expectations and consequences for learner behaviour, you build effective relationships. Such expectations may cover classroom etiquette and behaviour, group work, seating arrangements, the use of equipment and materials, and also classroom disruptions.

Assertive teacher behaviour also reassures learners that thoughts and messages are being passed on in an effective way. Assertive behaviour can be achieved by using erect posture, appropriate tone of voice depending on the current situation, and taking care not to ignore inappropriate behaviour.

A DIGNIFIED, CONSISTENT SYSTEM OF DISCIPLINE

4 factors:

how teachers regard their learners (spiritual dimension);

how they set up the classroom environment (physical dimension);

how skilfully they teach content (instructional dimension);

how well they address learner behaviour (managerial dimension).

Have few rules.

Behave like a mature adult – do not be too friendly.

Avoid showing attraction to the opposite sex.

Ensure that the few rules are adhered to: insist, for example, on politeness, punctuality, and prompt submission of work on an agreed date.

AVOID UNNECESSARY STRESS IN THE CLASSROOM

Avoid threats, shouting, sarcasm, cruel personal remarks, and favouritism.

Do NOT make fun of names or physical appearance.

TIME MANAGEMENT IN THE CLASSROOM

The goal of classroom management is to maintain order so that learning is possible. allocated time, instructional time, engaged time, and academic learning time.

Allocated time

Allocated time is the total time allotted for teaching, learning, and routine classroom procedures like attendance and announcements. Allocated time is also what appears on a learner's timetable:

e.g.: English 9:50-10:30 a.m. or Combined Science 1:15-2:00 p.m.

Instructional time

The time when teaching and learning actually takes place. Teachers maspend two or three minutes taking the register before their instruction begins.

Engaged time

Engaged time is also called time on task. During engaged time, learners are participating actively in learning activities—asking and responding to questions, completing worksheets and exercises, preparing presentations, etc.

Academic learning time

Academic learning time occurs when learners participate actively and are successful in learning activities.

Common mistakes in classroom behaviour management

These points are, to some extent, a reiteration of points made earlier.

In an effort to maintain order in the classroom, teachers can sometimes make the problems worse. Therefore, it is important to consider some of the basic mistakes commonly made when implementing classroom behaviour management strategies. For example, a common mistake made by teachers is to define the problem behaviour by how it looks, without considering its function.

Interventions are more likely to be effective when they are individualized and address the specific problem behaviour Two learners with similar misbehaviour may require entirely different intervention strategies if the behaviours are serving different functions.

Not every approach works for every learner and every age group. Teachers need to be flexible.

Another common mistake is for the teacher to become increasingly frustrated and negative when an approach is not working.

The teacher may raise their voice or increase adverse consequences in an effort to make an approach work. This type of interaction may impair the teacher-learner relationship. Instead of allowing this to happen, it is often better to simply try a new approach.

Inconsistency in expectations is an additional mistake that can lead to dysfunction in the classroom. Teachers must be consistent in order to ensure that learners understand that rules will be enforced. To avoid this, teachers should communicate expectations to learners clearly and be sufficiently committed to classroom management procedures to enforce them consistently.

ADDENDUM 3

STRATEGIC MANAGEMENT IN SCHOOL

Here are 6 topics to think about when planning your managing strategies.

I find a mnemonic comes in useful. A.C.I.D.A.L.

A.C.I.D.A.L.

anticipation

challenge – knowing the nature and extent of the challenge

interpretation of data and other information

decision-making

alignment of strategies

learning to apply the strategies in order to achieve lasting improvement.

Questions

Are you comfortable challenging your own and others' assumptions?

Can you get a diverse group to voluntarily agree a common vision?

Are you able to learn from your mistakes?

Let's look at each skill in turn.

ANTICIPATION

Many institutions today lack effective leadership.

Leaders are often poor at detecting threats and opportunities.

Effective strategic leaders are constantly vigilant, honing their ability to anticipate by scanning the environment for signals of change.

They also perform a regular SWOT analysis.

To improve your ability to anticipate:

Understand the challenges that beset others.

Conduct research through reading and by simple social analysis.

Use scenario planning to imagine various futures and prepare for the unexpected.

Look at a fast-growing rival and examine actions it has taken.

Attend conferences and events in the field of education.

CHALLENGE

Strategic thinkers always question the status quo.

They challenge their own and others' assumptions and encourage divergent points of view.

Only after careful reflection and examination of a problem do they take decisive action.

This requires patience, courage, and an open mind.

To improve your ability to challenge:

* Focus on the root causes of a problem rather than the symptoms.

* Encourage debate by holding meetings where open dialogue is expected and welcomed.

* Capture input from people not directly affected by a decision who may have a good perspective on the repercussions.

INTERPRET

Leaders who challenge invariably elicit complex and conflicting information. Therefore, it is necessary to interpret.

To improve your ability to interpret:

* When analysing ambiguous data, list at least three possible explanations for what you're observing and invite perspectives from diverse stakeholders.

* Force yourself to zoom in on the details and out to see the big picture.

* Supplement observation with quantitative analysis.

DECIDE

Leaders may have to make tough calls with incomplete information, and often they must do so quickly.

But strategic thinkers insist on multiple options at the outset and don't get prematurely locked into simplistic choices.

Strategic leaders must have the courage of their convictions—informed by a robust decision process.

To improve your ability to decide:

* Ask colleagues, especially senior staff, what other options they can suggest.

* Divide big decisions into pieces segments, better to understand component parts.

* Consider possible unintended consequences.

* Tailor your decision criteria to long-term versus short-term projects.

* Determine who needs to be directly involved and who can influence the success of your decision.

ALIGN

Strategic leaders must be adept at finding common ground. This requires active outreach. Success depends on proactive communication, trust building, and frequent engagement.

To improve your ability to align:

* Communicate early in order to offset negative criticism.

* Identify key internal and external stakeholders, and learn where they stand.

* Use structured and facilitated conversations to expose areas of misunderstanding or resistance.

* Reach out to resisters directly to understand their concerns and then address them.

* Be vigilant in monitoring stakeholders' positions during the roll out of your initiative or strategy.

* Recognize and reward colleagues who support team alignment.

LEARN

Strategic leaders are the focal point for organizational learning. They promote a culture of inquiry, and they search for the lessons in both successful and unsuccessful outcomes. They study failures—their own and their colleagues—in an open, constructive way.

To improve your ability to learn:

* Institute regular reviews.

* Reward colleagues who try something praiseworthy but fail in terms of outcomes.

* Conduct annual learning audits to see where decisions and team interactions may have fallen short.

* Identify initiatives that are not producing as expected and examine the root causes.

* Create a culture in which inquiry is valued and mistakes are viewed as learning opportunities.

This book, as was made clear at the beginning, is a prelude to a longer work on school improvement in all its aspects. Look out for this, and other forthcoming titles, on www.emmastern.com website.

The writing of this book is a small part of the fruits of more than fifty years of experience in various educational fields. To my many students and colleagues, in three continents, I owe thanks. Not all colleagues have been helpful but I thank them too; they showed me that change often means conflict, and I learned from them how to deal with opposition.

There is no such school as Glenfield School. Or, rather, it is many schools.

In the making of the book, in assisting me to bring it to the market place, I have to thank Nigel Pearson, Chief Editor of Emma Stern Publishing, and I extend my thanks to him without qualification or hesitation. This book is also your baby, Nigel.

www.ingramcontent.com/pod-product-compliance
Lightning Source LLC
Chambersburg PA
CBHW021212020426
42331CB00003B/332